History's Fearless Fighters

CONQUISTADORS

Rupert Matthews

Gareth Stevens
PUBLISHING

Please visit our website, **www.garethstevens.com**.
For a free color catalog of all our high-quality books, call toll free 1-800-542-2595 or fax 1-877-542-2596

Library of Congress Cataloging-in-Publication Data

Matthews, Rupert.
Conquistadors / by Rupert Matthews.
p. cm. — (History's fearless fighters)
Includes index.
ISBN 978-1-4824-3161-2 (pbk.)
ISBN 978-1-4824-3164-3 (6 pack)
ISBN 978-1-4824-3162-9 (library binding)
1. Soldiers — Spain — History — Juvenile literature.
2. Military art and science — History — Juvenile literature.
3. America — Discovery and exploration — Spanish — Juvenile literature.
I. Matthews, Rupert. II. Title.
E123.M38 2016
970.01'50922—d23

First Edition

Published in 2016 by
Gareth Stevens Publishing
111 East 14th Street, Suite 349
New York, NY 10003

© Alix Wood Books

Produced for Gareth Stevens by Alix Wood Books
Designed by Alix Wood
Editor: Eloise Macgregor

Photo credits:
Cover, 1, 3, 4, 5, 6, 7, 8, 9, 10, 12-13, 15 top, 17 top and bottom, 19 top, 22 top, 24, 25, 30, 34, 35, 36, 37 bottom left and right, 39, 40, 42 © Shutterstock; 14 © John Martin Perry; 15 bottom © Ginny Oshaben/ De Soto National Memorial, Florida; 16 © Kweniston; 17 middle © Jorge Louzao Penalva ; 18, 29 © Daderot; 19 bottom © The Field Museum Library; 20 © DollarPhotoClub; 21 © Biblioteca Museu Víctor Balaguer; 22 © Gold Museum, Bogota; 26 © Billy Hathorn; 28 top © Wehwalt; 28 bottom left © A.Skromnitsky; 28 bottom right © Christophe Meneboeuf; 31 top, 41 bottom © Brooklyn Museum; 33 © Architect of the Capitol; 37 top © Noradoa/Shutterstock; 43 top © Ethnological Museum, Berlin; 43 bottom © Despedes; remaining images are in the public domain

Printed in the United States of America
CPSIA compliance information: Batch #CS15GS: For further information contact Gareth Stevens, New York, New York at 1-800-542-2595.

Contents

The column of men armed with spears, shields, and knives wound down the mountain path to the forest below. Gold glinted from the earrings, headdresses, and bangles the nobles and commanders wore. In the trees men waited, wearing steel armor and armed with swords and pikes. As the column reached the trees a trumpet blared, and the men with swords charged forward. Their desire for gold would soon be satisfied.

In 1492 the Italian sailor Christopher Columbus crossed the Atlantic and landed in the Americas. He found a **fertile** land lived in by peoples who had a less advanced technology than that of Europe. Soon thousands of Spaniards and others were crossing to the Americas. Some came to farm, some to mine for minerals, but some came to conquer. They became known as **conquistadors**.

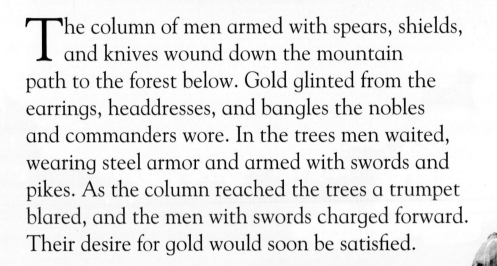

a statue of
Christopher Columbus

In 16th century Europe gold was rare and expensive. It was used to make valuable coins and used as money. In the Americas gold had no monetary value. It was used to make religious objects, or to show the high social rank of the person using it. The conquistadors wanted to get as much gold as they could because it was so valuable in Europe.

gold Inca ritual mask

The conquistadors were Christians. They thought that the gods and goddesses of the American peoples were worthless and false gods. They wanted to convert all the people in America to Christianity, even if that meant killing them first!

EXPLORING

The conquistadors were so eager to find gold and new people to **convert** to Christianity that they were willing to travel over great distances. Some marched across deserts, others sailed down rivers, and some climbed towering mountains. They traveled where no European had ever been before, and brought back amazing stories about the places they visited.

That's Fearless!

In 1527 Francisco Pizarro asked for conquistadors to volunteer to invade the Inca Empire. Only 13 men came forward, but he set off anyway.

Spanish Settlement

The Spanish **settlers** did not have an easy life. They were sometimes struck by disease or short of food. Large numbers of Spanish settlers died, but more kept arriving. The numbers of Europeans in the Americas grew steadily.

When Columbus landed on islands in the **West Indies** he thought he was on islands off the east coast of Asia! The Europeans did not know that North and South America existed in the ocean in between. He left some men at La Navidad in what is now Haiti to start building a town, but all those men were killed by the local Taino people. Four years later Columbus's brother founded the city of Santo Domingo, also on Haiti.

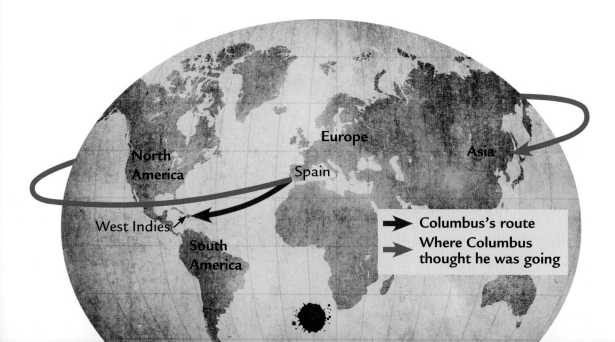

North America

Europe

Asia

Spain

West Indies

South America

➤ Columbus's route

➤ Where Columbus thought he was going

The first European settlement on the mainland was in what is now Venezuela. Nueva Cadiz was close to good fishing and pearl oysters. In 1541 a storm destroyed the entire town and it was abandoned. The first settlement in the south was in Buenos Aires, now the capital of Argentina. It was originally called "Ciudad de Nuestra Señora Santa María del Buen Ayre!" It was abandoned after a war with local Charrúa people, then refounded in 1580.

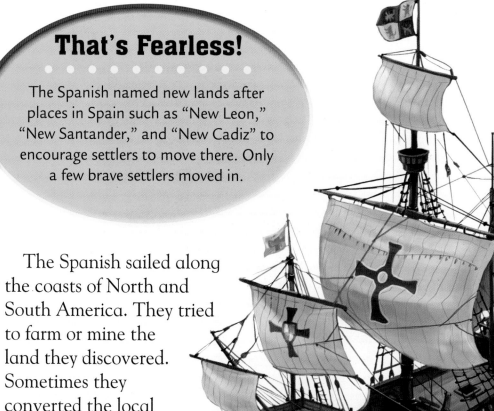

That's Fearless!

The Spanish named new lands after places in Spain such as "New Leon," "New Santander," and "New Cadiz" to encourage settlers to move there. Only a few brave settlers moved in.

The Spanish sailed along the coasts of North and South America. They tried to farm or mine the land they discovered. Sometimes they converted the local people to Christianity and paid them to work. In other places they used local people as **slaves**.

Columbus's biggest ship, the *Santa Maria*, was less than 75 feet (23 m) long!

Indigenous Peoples

When Columbus arrived there were around 30 million people living in the New World. Hundreds of different nations and tribes had their own language, culture, and way of life. The arrival of Europeans was a disaster. Within 150 years the native **population** had been cut by about 90 percent, mostly by diseases such as smallpox. Native Americans had no resistance to European diseases.

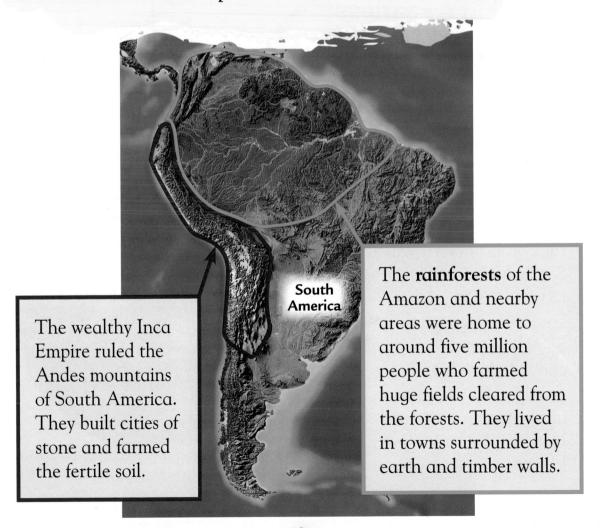

South America

The wealthy Inca Empire ruled the Andes mountains of South America. They built cities of stone and farmed the fertile soil.

The **rainforests** of the Amazon and nearby areas were home to around five million people who farmed huge fields cleared from the forests. They lived in towns surrounded by earth and timber walls.

In the mountains of western North America peoples such as the Yokuts hunted animals and gathered seeds to store through the winter.

The plains of central North America were home to peoples who hunted **bison**, fished in the rivers and gathered wild plants. These included the Apache, Teyas, Comanche, and Wichita.

The dry lands to the south of North America were home to peoples such as the Navajo who grew crops in **irrigated** fields and hunted wild animals.

North America

Central America

In Central America there were large populations of farmers. The Aztecs formed a single, powerful empire based in the city of Tenochtitlán (now Mexico City), which had a population of about 40,000.

Further south the Maya farmed the dense jungle lands and were divided into a number of smaller states.

Religion

The Spanish conquistadors came from a Christian country. Some were good men, others were violent and bloodthirsty. They believed it was their duty to convert people to Christianity. They thought the local people's beliefs were evil.

The Aztecs and Maya believed **sacrifice** was essential to keep their gods healthy. Some gods required sacrifices of flowers, eggs, or vegetables burned on an **altar**. Greater gods needed blood sacrifices. Priests cut their arms or chests to pour blood on the altar. Nobles slit their tongues to provide blood.

That's Fearless!

Some Aztec gods, such as Tlaloc, god of rain (left), and Huitzilopochtli, god of war, demanded human sacrifice. Several thousand people were killed each year by having their hearts cut out and offered to the gods!

PEDRO DE CÓRDOBA

The Spanish priest Pedro de Córdoba went to live on the island of Santo Domingo in 1510. He dedicated his life to converting the local peoples to Christianity. He wrote a book designed to help other missionaries work in the Americas. He campaigned against cruel treatment of the locals by Spanish settlers, especially the way they were forced to become slaves.

The Incas of South America worshiped the sun god, Inti. They believed gold was sacred to Inti as it looked like the golden rays of the sun. Statues of solid gold decorated Inca temples, and sheets of gold covered the walls.

A reconstruction of a gold panel that hung above an altar at the Inca temple, Qurikancha

The peoples of the plains, such as the Apache, believed powerful spirits walked the Earth. Ceremonies involving dances, ball games, and sacrifices allowed some humans to talk to the spirits. They could gain their good will or learn what the spirits wanted.

The Navajo and other peoples believed that certain men were touched by the gods and spirits. These men had to learn up to 60 special ceremonies. Each one lasted four days and involved songs, dances, and making special objects. If these ceremonies were carried out properly, the gods were satisfied and the people would live well.

Francisco de Córdoba

Francisco de Córdoba set out from Cuba to explore the lands to the south. He had no idea what he would find. In fact he stumbled across a great city built by the Maya.

Córdoba moved to the Americas in about 1509 and by 1517 he was living in Cuba. Córdoba owned a large farming estate, worked by local slaves. He decided to search for lands that he could raid for more slaves. He took three ships and 110 men and headed south.

After a month, Córdoba sighted land near what is now Cancun on the Yucatán Peninsula. As he explored inland, he found a vast stone city. A huge pyramid dominated the city, topped by a temple.

The typical Mayan temple, the Temple of the Warriors in the jungle near Cancun

Up to this point the Spaniards had only found small villages of wooden huts. Córdoba called the city "Gran Cairo," after the city in Egypt that had pyramids nearby. After a short fight the Spaniards set sail again.

After sailing along the coast for several days, Córdoba led his men ashore to find fresh water. They were quickly surrounded by an army of about 5,000 Maya! When a leader gave a shout, the Maya attacked. Córdoba led his men back to their boats, using their steel swords and armor to beat off the Maya. Córdoba and the survivors eventually got back to Cuba. Córdoba himself had been wounded seven times in the fighting and died of his wounds a week later.

That's Fearless!

The battle with the Maya at Champotón was fierce. In all 50 Spaniards were killed and 40 were wounded. Two of the Spaniards were captured, and they were later sacrificed to the Maya gods.

STARTING THE HUNT FOR GOLD

Córdoba and his men told people in Cuba what they had seen. The reports of a large city, the organized people, and the gold jewelry convinced the Spaniards on Cuba that a vast wealth of gold would be found on the mainland. One of the men who heard the stories was named Hernán Cortés.

Spanish Infantry

Most conquistador soldiers marched and fought on foot. These men were responsible for winning the battles. Their equipment and the way they fought gave them an advantage over the local enemy.

Many conquistadors went into battle as rodeleros. Rodeleros wore an iron helmet, shield, and breastplate. A long steel sword was their main weapon. They also had a dagger. In battle they stood in dense formations side by side, several ranks deep.

That's Fearless!

In 1536 Juan Pizarro led 70 Spanish horsemen out of the besieged city of Cuzco to get help. Juan was hit on the head by a sling stone. He rode on although he felt dizzy. Four days later he dropped dead from brain damage!

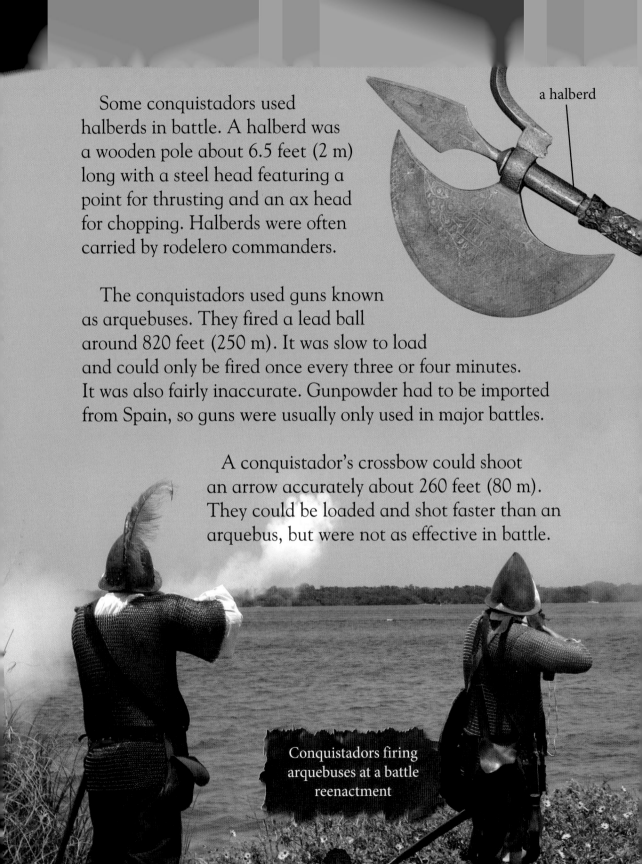

Some conquistadors used halberds in battle. A halberd was a wooden pole about 6.5 feet (2 m) long with a steel head featuring a point for thrusting and an ax head for chopping. Halberds were often carried by rodelero commanders.

a halberd

The conquistadors used guns known as arquebuses. They fired a lead ball around 820 feet (250 m). It was slow to load and could only be fired once every three or four minutes. It was also fairly inaccurate. Gunpowder had to be imported from Spain, so guns were usually only used in major battles.

A conquistador's crossbow could shoot an arrow accurately about 260 feet (80 m). They could be loaded and shot faster than an arquebus, but were not as effective in battle.

Conquistadors firing arquebuses at a battle reenactment

Animal Power

Conquistador armies were famous for their ability to march long distances quickly. This gave them an advantage over the Native American armies which moved more slowly. Their speed was partly due to the horses brought from Europe, but other animals played a part as well.

Around 10 percent of conquistadors fought as **cavalry** on horseback. They wore steel helmets and body armor, and fought with a sword or lance. The sheer power of a horse galloping at high speed was enough to smash a path through enemy formations, even before the sword was used.

That's Fearless!

At the Battle of Puná in 1531 Francisco Pizarro led a charge of 27 cavalry against an army of 3,000. The enemy had never seen horses before, so they simply fled.

When he arrived in the Americas, Columbus was astonished to learn that nobody there used horses. On his second voyage he took some horses with him. Every later Spanish expedition took more horses over the ocean. The Iberian Spanish horses were fairly short and stocky with strong muscles and great endurance.

The conquistadors used war dogs in battle. A breed of dog named the "Alano Español" was used in Spain to hunt wild cattle and wild boar. The dogs were large, with very strong jaws. They were well known for their courage. The dogs were trained to attack and were used to kill enemy soldiers in battle.

THE DEADLY DONKEY

Conquistadors took thousands of donkeys on campaign with them. The donkeys were used to carry food, weapons, and other supplies. This meant that the conquistador armies could move very quickly even over rough country.

The Armies from the Americas

The armies that the conquistadors faced were large, disciplined, and well trained. However, they did not have firearms or metal weapons which was a disadvantage when fighting the Spanish. They could still defeat invaders in a battle, though.

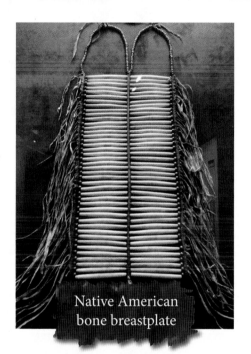

Native American bone breastplate

Armor was made of layers of cotton cloth stitched together. Wooden plates were sewn into areas that did not need to bend. Breastplates could be made of strips of bone or shell. The armor worked against local weapons, but Spanish steel swords cut straight through it.

Shields were made of jointed wooden pieces covered in leather. They could stop swords and spears, but were no use against firearms.

Helmets were carved out of blocks of wood and padded inside with thick layers of cotton. Some were covered with copper to make them stronger. Senior officers' and nobles' helmets were covered with gold.

That's Fearless!

At Punta Quemada in 1525 Francisco Pizarro and 30 of his men were ambushed by over 300 Quitian warriors. Pizarro held off the attack until help arrived, but he was wounded seven times during the fight!

Native American weapons included slings, javelins, and bows that could hit the enemy at a distance. Up close, spears and clubs were used. Some clubs were studded with razor-sharp blades made from the stone **obsidian**. Obsidian was also used to make knives and short swords. None of these weapons could get through Spanish steel armor.

The Inca Empire had an army of about 200,000 men in 1525. In battle, the **slingers** and **archers** would attack first. Then men with clubs and obsidian knives attacked. Often a force would surprise attack the enemy at the side or rear. If the army retreated, men with long spears would form a solid hedge of spikes to protect the wounded as they were carried to safety.

Mayan
obsidian knife

FIERCE AZTECS

The size of the Aztec army could be 700,000 men, but was usually much smaller. The army was led by a parade of priests carrying statues of the gods. Drums and smoke signals were used to pass messages and orders between commanders. Men who performed well in battle were invited to join warrior societies named after ferocious animals such as the jaguar or the eagle.

Aztec warriors carrying clubs
studded with obsidian blades

Hernán Cortés

Hernán Cortés conquered the Aztec Empire. The vast treasures that he brought back to Spain convinced many young men that they could become rich if they went to the Americas.

Cortés was from a poor, noble Spanish family. His cousin was made Governor of Hispaniola and gave Cortés a job in government, a large farm, and slaves to work it for him. In 1518 Cortés was put in command of ships carrying 500 men and 13 horses to Mexico. Hearing of a powerful Aztec empire there, Cortés sent a message asking to meet the ruler, Moctezuma. Moctezuma refused. Cortés set out for the Aztec capital, Tenochtitlán, anyway.

When Cortés learned that Spaniards had been killed by the Aztecs, he took Moctezuma prisoner and forced him to hand over huge quantities of gold and silver. When the Aztecs became unhappy, Cortés had Moctezuma murdered and then fled.

Cortés sent for more men and raised armies from local **allies**. He captured Tenochtitlán in 1521. Cortés ordered his men to destroy the Aztec temples and palaces. He built a new city in the Spanish style. Between 1521 and 1528 Cortés ruled the old Aztec Empire on behalf of the King of Spain. He stopped rebellions, divided the land up between conquistadors, converted locals to Christianity, and conquered nearby lands.

That's Fearless!

When Cortés arrived on the coast of Mexico he sank all his ships so that he could not return. He had to defeat the Aztecs or die.

HOME TO SPAIN

In 1528 Cortés was accused of cheating the King of Spain out of taxes. He went back to Spain but the King found him innocent.

A painting of Cortés fighting his way back into Tenochtitlán

Legendary Cities of Gold

S ome conquistadors were looking for land to farm or people to convert to Christianity. But most were looking to become rich. That meant getting hold of gold, and they did not care where they found it or how they got it. There were many legends about where there was gold.

EL DORADO

"El dorado" is Spanish for "the golden one." The term referred to a custom of the Muisca people of Colombia, where their king is covered in gold dust and then dove into a sacred lake. The conquistadors believed this king must rule a wealthy empire. In 1535 an expedition went up the Meta River to find El Dorado, but found nothing. In 1537 an army of 800 conquistadors invaded the Muisca. The amount of gold they found was small, so the search for El Dorado went on. Conquistadors even tried to drain the Muisca's sacred lake using buckets to search for the gold! English explorer Sir Walter Raleigh searched Guyana for El Dorado. As late as 1780 expeditions were still searching South America looking for El Dorado. Hundreds of men died trying, but nobody found the mysterious El Dorado because it had never existed!

An ancient Columbian statue of the golden king "El Dorado" on his raft

SEVEN CITIES OF GOLD

From about 1520, Spaniards in what is now Mexico began hearing stories about rich cities to the north. The stories were passed on by local people who said that far to the north beyond the deserts of what is now the southwest of North America there were lands of wealth and plenty. These tales may simply have referred to the farming settlements of the pueblo peoples. Soon the stories about a land of plentiful food became stories about a land of plentiful gold, known as the "Seven Cities of Gold." The more the Spaniards asked about gold, the more the stories began to involve gold. The cities were never found as they never existed!

QUIVIRA

Francisco Vásquez de Coronado heard tales of a rich city called Quivira. He led an expedition but found a farming village instead. Later conquistadors thought he had been tricked, the real Quivira must be nearby. Francisco Leyba Bonilla and Antonio de Humana led an expedition. The only survivor, a Mexican, said he left the expedition after the Spaniards began arguing with each other. In 1601 Don Juan de Oñate looked for Quivira in Kansas. He only found some Wichita villages. Diego Dionisio de Penalosa led the last expedition in 1662.

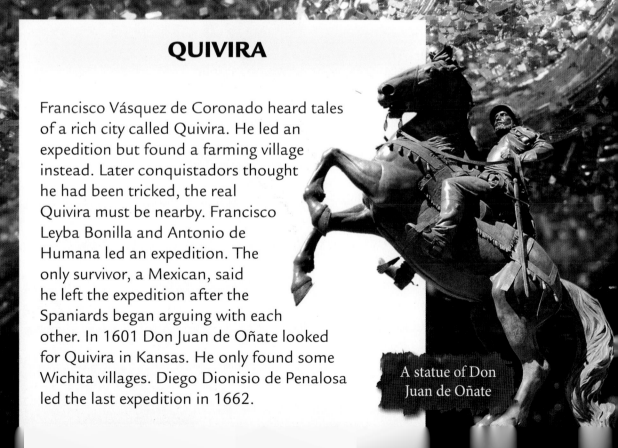

A statue of Don Juan de Oñate

Silver, Diamonds, and Spice

Gold was not the only thing that the Spaniards searched for in the Americas. Silver and diamonds, and cinnamon trees were all of value to the Spanish conquistadors. They also searched for missing Spanish settlers.

Stunning mystical mountains in Patagonia

TRAPANANDA

Stories about a prosperous city named Trapananda began to be heard in the 1590s. The city was said to be somewhere in Patagonia in South America. It was believed to be inhabited by a group of Inca who had fled the Spanish conquistadors. The Inca found a secluded valley with a very narrow entrance. The valley was believed to be between two mountains, one with a mine producing diamonds and the other producing gold. Sometimes it is described as an enchanted city inhabited by giants or ghosts!

ANTILLIA

An old Spanish legend told of a group of several thousand Spaniards who fled to a land west of the Atlantic Ocean in the year 734. The Spaniards, led by seven bishops, were fleeing a Muslim invasion of Spain. They settled in Antillia, and built several towns and villages. For a while they kept in touch with Spain by ship, but gradually contact was lost. When America was discovered many Spaniards thought it was Antillia. Several expeditions set out looking for the towns, but they were never found.

LA CANELA

Legend had it that La Canela was a land east of the Andes where cinnamon trees grew. In the 16th century cinnamon bark was a very valuable spice grown only in southern India. The story began after the discovery of trees that smelled like cinnamon in the eastern Andes in 1539. The trees did not produce the cinnamon spice.

Ciudad Perdida (Spanish for "Lost City") in the Colombian jungle can only be reached after a six-day walk through the jungle!

PAITITI

In 1570 Juan Álvarez Maldonado said local Incas had told him that huge amounts of silver had once been mined near the city of Paititi. This city was said to be at a secret location somewhere in the dense rainforest east of the Andes mountains. In the 20th century ruins of Inca fortresses were found in the rainforest at Beni, Riberalta, and Kimbiri, but no silver mines are known in these areas.

Vasquez de Coronado

Francisco Vásquez de Coronado set out to find and conquer the legendary Seven Cities of Gold. Despite fighting many battles and exploring large areas of what is now America, he never found any gold.

In 1539 Coronado was **governor** of New Galicia, northwest Mexico. A **friar** arrived from the unexplored north, saying that another friar had been killed while trying to convert people in the city of Cíbola to Christianity. He said that Cíbola was a large, wealthy city and he had been told that seven cities rich in gold lay further north.

Coronado decided to attack Cíbola in revenge, and search for the Seven Cities of Gold. He took 400 Spanish soldiers, 2,000 local armed men, four friars, and a large number of cooks and servants.

The expedition eventually reached Cíbola, in what is now New Mexico. They found the pueblos of the Zuni people. The buildings were impressive, but there was no gold and little food.

Coronado spent several months exploring the area. One day a man from a distant tribe was brought to Coronado by the Zuni. He told Coronado that the cities were called Quivira and lay to the east. Coronado set off with the man acting as his guide. There, Coronado and his men met the Teyas tribe who told Coronado he was going the wrong way, Quivira lay to the north.

That's Fearless!

Coronado ordered his lieutenant García López de Cárdenas to take men to search for a large river said to be north of Quivira. After marching across a desert for 20 days Cárdenas arrived at the Grand Canyon.

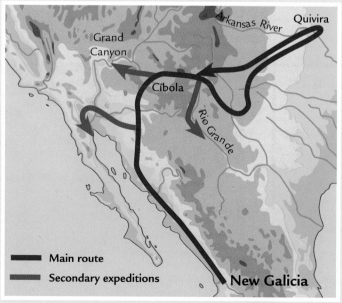

Grand Canyon

Arkansas River   Quivira

Cíbola

Rio Grande

New Galicia

Main route

Secondary expeditions

FINDING QUIVIRA

When Coronado reached Quivira he just found farming villages. The nearby towns were the same. There was no city and no gold. Coronado was furious and ordered his men to kill his guide!

Real Gold and Silver

In many areas of the Americas, the conquistadors found local people using gold and silver as jewelry or as ritual objects. The precious items were quickly stolen by the conquistadors. Once they had taken all the precious items, the Spanish began looking for where the gold and silver came from.

According to an Inca legend, the ruler Huayna Capac discovered the silver mines of Potosi in about 1462. When the Spaniards took over the mines they increased production using the local people as workers. Some were paid, others were forced to work without pay. Between 1556 and 1783 the Spaniards **exported** 45,000 tons of silver from Potosi! The famous mountain of silver at Potosi is now about one third of a mile (500 m) shorter than it was in 1550 due to the amount of silver **ore** removed!

A Spanish coin made from silver from the Potosi mine

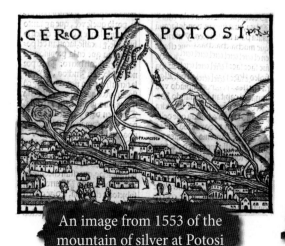

An image from 1553 of the mountain of silver at Potosi

A much smaller Cerro Rico, today. Cerro Rico means "wealthy mountain."

GOLD IN THE HILLS

The Andes Mountains contain some of the richest gold and silver mines in the world. The Incas found most of their gold in the sand in or near rivers. Gold from the rock was washed down by rainwater into the rivers, then trapped in sand. Using European techniques the Spaniards could get gold directly from the rock instead. The world's second largest gold mine today is Yanacocha, in the Andes. It produces about 11,000 pounds (50,000 kg) of pure gold every year!

A cup made from Peruvian gold

Spaniards looking to exploit the Aztec's gold mines were quickly disappointed. Mines in the Oaxaca Valley produced an ore that contained only small amounts of gold. The Spaniards soon found it cost more to mine the gold than they could get by selling it. The Aztecs had mined the gold to make important objects so they did not mind the high price. In 1521 Spanish miners discovered a new area of gold ore that they called "El Oro." With their technology they could reach gold that the Aztecs could not. Soon they were producing about 750 pounds (340 kg) of gold each year.

Francisco Pizarro

Francisco Pizarro conquered the great Inca Empire in 1532. He looted more gold than any other single man has ever stolen from anyone.

Pizarro was the son of a soldier. He did not attend school so he could not read or write, but his father did teach him how to use weapons and the importance of discipline and command. In 1509 he left Spain to go to the Americas to earn a living as a soldier.

In 1524 Pizarro formed a partnership with a fellow soldier, Diego de Almagro, and a priest named Hernando de Luque. They planned to explore the south, convert people to Christianity and grab as much gold or silver as they could. Pizarro persuaded 168 men to join him, 62 of which were cavalry. They marched into the Inca Empire in 1532.

A statue of Francisco Pizarro

Pizarro lured the Inca ruler Atahualpa into a meeting, then killed his guards and made him a prisoner. Seeing the Spaniards ripping golden jewelry from the Inca bodies, Atahualpa offered to buy his freedom with gold. He said he would fill a room with gold, then fill it twice again with silver. He kept his promise. Instead of freeing him, however, Pizarro put Atahualpa on trial for being a pagan and a murderer, and for plotting the death of the Spaniards. He was executed on July 26, 1533.

Atahualpa

GOVERNOR PIZARRO

Having defeated several Inca armies, Pizarro declared himself to be Governor of the Inca empire on behalf of the King of Spain. He began organizing the empire and sent out men to explore and conquer new areas. His friend Almagro resented being given orders by Pizarro. He started a rebellion, but Pizarro had him killed.

That's Fearless!

In 1541 Pizarro was enjoying a banquet in his palace in Lima. Suddenly 20 armed men burst in, led by Almagro's son. The guests fled. Pizarro grabbed his sword and killed two men before he was attacked. As he lay dying Pizarro drew a cross on the floor with his own blood and gasped for help from Christ.

Hernando de Soto

Hernando de Soto was a professional soldier who fought in several conquistador campaigns in Central and South America. He is best known for his huge expedition into North America.

De Soto became rich helping Pizarro to conquer the Inca Empire. He then read reports from men who had been to North America. He believed that the continent contained a civilization as rich and large as the Aztec or Inca. De Soto decided to go and find it.

In May 1539 de Soto landed in Tampa Bay, Florida, with 620 men and 220 horses. The expedition included priests, farmers, and engineers as well as soldiers. For several weeks the expedition marched north up the Florida coast. They spent the winter at Anhaica, where the remains of their camp have been found.

That's Fearless!

De Soto was the first Spaniard to meet the Inca ruler Atahualpa. He walked alone with an Inca interpreter into the middle of the Inca army of 80,000 men.

They went north through what is now Georgia and the Carolinas before turning west into Tennessee and Alabama. In central Alabama the Spaniards entered the territory of Chief Tuskaloosa and demanded food. Tuskaloosa led de Soto into an **ambush** at the fortified town of Mabila. About 200 Spaniards were killed and 150 injured, while around 2,500 locals were killed.

De Soto then led his men west until they reached the banks of the Mississippi River. After a month building boats they crossed the river, and moved through Arkansas, Oklahoma, and Texas. Finding nothing, the next spring they returned to the Mississippi, probably in Louisiana. De Soto then fell ill with a fever and died.

LOST

With de Soto dead, the survivors had no food, and only a vague idea of where they were. They decided to give up. After trying to find a route overland to Mexico they built boats and traveled down the Mississippi and along the coast to safety at the Spanish settlement of Panuco.

De Soto arriving at the Mississippi

The conquistadors had a huge impact on the Americas, and on Europe. Their armies destroyed empires. The introduction of Christianity wiped out local religions. In Europe the increase in available gold and silver affected the value of their money.

Huge amounts of silver and gold flooded into Europe from the Americas. The coins people had became less valuable because gold and silver became less precious. Prices rose, but wages did not, so many people became poor.

The Spanish kings took 20 percent of wealth found in the Americas, and became the richest monarchs in Europe. They spent the money on armies and navies to conquer their enemies. King Philip II paid for the mighty Spanish Armada which tried to invade England.

The Spanish Armada attacking England

The Native Americans smoked tobacco in their rituals or to symbolize the sealing of an agreement. Europeans soon began smoking tobacco for enjoyment. Smoking tobacco became enormously popular, until the 20th century when it was realized that smoking caused fatal lung diseases.

Food Swaps

The conquistadors took European foods to the Americas and brought American foods to Europe.

European Foods to America:
Wheat, barley, oranges, lemons, apples, onions, coffee, rice, milk, cheese, cattle, sheep, goats, pigs

American Foods to Europe:
Sweet corn, potato, chocolate, chili, vanilla, tomato, peanuts

SPREADING DISEASE

The peoples of the Americas had no **immunity** to European diseases such as smallpox, measles, or chickenpox. Many died in a very short period of time. In some areas over 95 percent of the local population died in less than a year. Not only did people die, so did societies. States broke up, religions collapsed, and lands were left derelict. Some American diseases spread to Europe, but these were less serious.

Long-Term legacy

It is now nearly 500 years since the conquistadors fought across the Americas, but the impact of their battles can still be seen. The modern world of today would be very different if it were not for the conquistadors.

CHRISTIANITY

The conquistadors forced people to convert to Christianity. They did not value the gods that were worshiped in America, and particularly disliked the idea of human sacrifice. The old temples were destroyed and new Christian churches were built.

SPEAKING SPANISH

When the conquistadors arrived hundreds of different languages were spoken in the Americas. Today Spanish is spoken all across the areas conquered by the Spanish conquistadors. Many people still speak their own local language as well, but schools teach children how to speak Spanish. This means that people from Argentina can talk easily to people from Mexico.

A ruined Inca temple near Cuzco, Peru

NEW NATIONS

When the Spanish conquered an area they swept away the old empires and states that had existed before them. Those old states had fought long and brutal wars against each other. The Spanish brought peace and stability, although they enslaved the peoples to achieve it. The Spanish divided their lands up to make them easier to govern, using mountains or rivers as borders. Those divisions now create the borders of countries such as Argentina, Mexico, Guatemala, and Colombia.

The river Usumacinta separates Mexico and Guatemala

MONEY

Before the Spaniards arrived, money was not used in the Americas. People swapped goods instead. The Spanish introduced money as a way of buying things. They also introduced more modern farming methods and industry.

THANKS CONQUISTADORS

Why would we have to thank the conquistadors for pizza? It was invented by a baker in Naples, Italy in about 1750. He was baking the traditional cheese-topped bread when he decided to use some sauce from tomatoes that had been brought to Europe by the Spaniards. It was delicious. The pizza was born!

Francisco de Orellana

Francisco de Orellana became famous almost by accident when he explored the entire length of the mighty Amazon River. Although he was famous in his lifetime, later historians decided he had lied. Only in the 21st century did it become clear that Orellana told the truth about his adventures.

In 1541 Orellana was second in command of an expedition trying to find cinnamon said to grow in the east. When the expedition reached the Coca River, the men built a large boat named *San Pedro*. Orellana and 50 men were told to explore down the river for a couple of weeks, then come back.

The current was too strong to sail back! Orellana continued downstream to explore the river and reach the sea. They soon found themselves traveling though large towns built of wood, surrounded by strong wooden walls, and fields of crops and forest.

AMAZONS

In June 1542 Orellana and his men were attacked by women armed with bows and arrows. Orellana called them "Amazons" after the warrior women of ancient Greek legend. The name was later given to the river and the area.

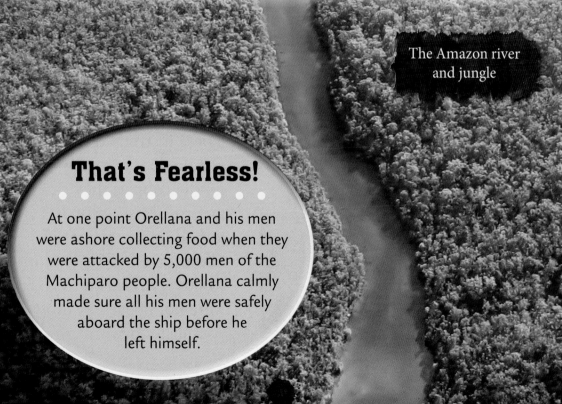

Orellana and his men reached the sea eight months later. They sailed north to a Spanish settlement and then Orellana sailed to Spain. King Charles gave him ships and an army to conquer the great cities of the Amazon. The fleet was wrecked in a storm and Orellana died of fever.

By the time Europeans returned to the Amazon in the 1650s there were no cities, towns, and fields. Instead there was endless forest with a few small tribes of perhaps 200,000 people. People thought Orellana had been lying about what he found. In the 21st century **archaeologists** found the remains of the wooden towns and cities that Orellana had described. We now know that over 5 million people had lived in the area in 1542, but that European diseases had wiped out almost the whole population.

The Amazon river and jungle

That's Fearless!

At one point Orellana and his men were ashore collecting food when they were attacked by 5,000 men of the Machiparo people. Orellana calmly made sure all his men were safely aboard the ship before he left himself.

Conquistador Timeline

The Conquistadors conquered vast territories and fought many battles, sometimes outnumbered by 100 to 1. They converted people to Christianity, enslaved entire nations, and changed the world forever. All this was achieved in less than a hundred years.

- **1492**
Christopher Columbus lands on the islands off the coast of Central America that we now call the West Indies.

- **1511**
First Spanish settlement is founded on Cuba.

1510

1490

- **1509**
A permanent Spanish town is founded on Jamaica, named New Seville.

- **1512**
The Laws of Burgos are passed in Spain. These instructed the conquistadors to convert all the peoples they met to Christianity. It forbade slavery, but did allow forced labor similar to slavery. The laws were not obeyed by all conquistadors.

Montego Bay

New Seville

Kingston

JAMAICA

1517

Francisco Hernández de Córdoba leads an expedition to the Yucatán Peninsula where he becomes the first European to see a large city built of stone in the Americas. He is attacked by a local Maya army.

1515

1518

Hernán Cortés sails to Mexico with a small army. He discovers a land of wealth and civilization, the most powerful being the Aztec.

1520

1520

Cortés conquers the Aztec Empire, destroys their capital city, Tenochtitlán and divides the empire up under Spanish ownership. He returns to Spain with vast amounts of treasure.

1526

Francisco Pizarro leads an exploration along the Pacific coast to the edge of the Inca Empire.

Inca ruler Huayna Capac

1529

Smallpox sweeps through South America, killing much of the population. Among those to die is Huayna Capac, ruler of the Inca Empire.

1532

Pizarro tricks the Inca ruler Atahualpa into captivity and steals gold and silver before murdering him. Pizarro is murdered by one of his men in a feud.

1530

A gold statue of Atahualpa, Cuzco, Peru

That's Fearless!

At the Battle of Ollantaytambo in 1537, Hernando Pizarro led a charge of 70 mounted conquistadors against an Inca army of 30,000 men. He only gave up when the horses got stuck in mud up to their bellies!

1537

After many wars, the Inca ruler Manco Inca retreats to the dense forest city of Vilcabamba. He is killed by the Spanish in 1545 and was succeeded as ruler of Vilcabamba by his son Sayri Tupac.

1536

The city of Buenos Aires is founded in what is now Argentina. Also in 1536 Spanish ships explore the coast of Florida. Also in 1536 four survivors return to Mexico after nine years traveling through Texas, Mississippi, New Mexico, and Arizona. They bring tales of seven rich cities, rumored to exist somewhere in North America.

1539

Hernando de Soto's army lands in Florida to search for a civilized and wealthy empire that he believes lies in North America. Over the next three years the expedition searched but found no gold or silver.

- **1540**
Francisco Vásquez de Coronado sets out with a small army to punish the people of Cíbola for killing a Spanish friar and to search for the Seven Cities of Gold.

- **1545**
An epidemic fever sweeps through Mexico and Central America, killing about 60 percent of the population. Another outbreak of fever in 1580 killed about half of those left alive. By 1623 only 300,000 Native Americans were left alive in Mexico and Central America from about 27 million in 1500.

1540

- **1541**
Francisco de Orellana starts his journey down the Amazon river. Orellana then sails to Spain to recruit an army to conquer the area, but dies before he can do so.

1570

- **1572**
The Spanish declare war on Tupac Amaru, ruler of the Incas of Vilcabamba. Tupac Amaru is captured and the city of Vilcabamba is destroyed. The last remnants of the Inca Empire have ceased to exist.

A water spout at the ruins of Vilcabamba

What Do You Know?

Can you answer these questions about the conquistadors?

1. What is a halberd?

2. In which year did Christopher Columbus land on American soil?

3. Who or what was Inti?

4. What was conquistador armor made from?

5. What was Inca and Aztec armor made from?

6. What animal did the conquistadors use to carry their food and supplies?

7. Why did Cortés take Moctezuma prisoner?

8. Name a food now eaten in Europe that originated in the Americas.

9. What religion did most conquistadors follow?

10. What stone did Native Americans make their blades from?

Answers on page 48

Further Information

Books

Baquedano, Elizabeth. *Aztec* (Eyewitness). New York, NY: Dorling Kindersley, 2011.

Clarke, Cariona. *Aztecs.* (Usborne Beginners). London, UK: Usborne, 2007.

Deary, Terry. *The Incredible Incas* (Horrible Histories). Danbury, CT: Scholastic Publishing, 2008.

MacDonald, Fiona. *Avoid Becoming an Aztec Sacrifice!* (Danger Zone). Brighton, England: Salariya Book Company, 2002.

Websites

BBC website on Christopher Columbus with games and facts
http://www.bbc.co.uk/schools/primaryhistory/famouspeople/christopher_columbus/

Ducksters website with information about the conquistadors
http://www.ducksters.com/biography/explorers/spanish_conquistadores.php

Glossary

allies People who cooperate together to achieve an objective, usually fighting on the same side in a war.

altar A stone or table placed in a temple or church to receive offerings to a god or goddess.

ambush A surprise attack, usually launched from a hiding place.

archaeologists People who study ruins and ancient artifacts dug up out of the ground in order to study the past.

bison A large cattle-like animal that lives wild on the grasslands of North America.

cavalry Soldiers who fight while riding horses.

conquistadors The name given to Spanish soldiers who fought against the native peoples of the Americas.

convert To persuade a person to change from one religion to another.

exported Carried from one place to another in order to sell.

fertile An area of land that is able to produce plenty of crops.

governor The chief government official of a province or other large area.

immunity The ability of a person not to catch a disease, or to suffer the effects of that disease only mildly.

irrigated Land that is provided with water artificially by humans, often by digging ditches to carry water from a nearby river or stream.

obsidian A form of rock found near volcanoes that is similar to glass.

ore A type of rock that contains large amounts of metal.

population All the people living in a particular place or area.

rainforest A dense forest that grows in tropical areas where rain is particularly heavy.

sacrifice An offering made to a god.

settlers People who leave one country to go to live in another.

slaves People forced to work without pay and who are often beaten or otherwise mistreated.

West Indies The islands that lie east of Mexico, between North America and South America.

Index

Answers to Quiz

1. a weapon consisting of a steel blade mounted on a long pole
2. 1492
3. the sun god of the Inca
4. steel
5. cotton and wood
6. donkeys
7. because the Aztecs had killed some Spaniards
8. sweet corn, potato, vanilla, chocolate, tomato, peanuts, or chili
9. Christianity
10. obsidian